Original title:
Tropical Sighs

Copyright © 2025 Creative Arts Management OÜ
All rights reserved.

Author: Julian Prescott
ISBN HARDBACK: 978-1-80581-591-4
ISBN PAPERBACK: 978-1-80581-118-3
ISBN EBOOK: 978-1-80581-591-4

Gold Dust Over Coral Reefs

Bubbles rise, fish dance in a row,
A clownfish giggles, stealing the show.
Sunlight sparkles, like stars on the sea,
Jellyfish waltz, quite carefree and free.

A turtle drags, lost in his dream,
While dolphins plot, the best prank scheme.
Coral pink, blue, a riotous sight,
Nature's confetti, what a delight!

Serenity Found in Ocean Depths

Octopus juggles shells with finesse,
While sea cucumbers play dress to impress.
A hermit crab moves in a borrowed shoe,
In this underwater play, nothing's askew.

Starfish ponder, 'What's life all about?'
Seahorses giggle, wrapping in a clout.
The seaweed sways, like a dancer's spree,
In the quiet depth, pure absurdity!

Mirage of the Infinite Horizon

Fish wear sunglasses, looking so cool,
Seagulls squawk jokes, ruling the pool.
A whale hums loudly, off-key yet bold,
Sunsets are raves, the colors unfold.

Sandy iguanas sipping on tea,
While crabs try twerking, so fun to see!
A mermaid chuckles, hair full of seaweed,
This endless expanse, oh what a breed!

A Symphony of Shells and Sand

Conch shells trumpet, sounding the call,
Coconuts giggle, they're having a ball.
Sandcastles shout, 'We rule this shore!'
Seashells play tunes, who could ask for more?

Crabs in top hats, ready for tea,
With starfish as guests, quite posh you see!
The beaches come alive, laughter and cheer,
In this wild ballet, joy's always near!

Hushed Secrets of the Distant Shore

The coconut laughed, cracked up in glee,
As the waves tickled toes, wild and free.
Seagulls wearing sun hats, looking so bright,
Were squawking out jokes, oh what a sight!

Palm trees swayed, looking dapper and spry,
Whispering secrets of the crabby pie.
Shells danced on the sand, in a conga line,
While fish flipped their fins, shouting, 'This is fine!'

Elysium Skies over Crystal Waters

Clouds were cotton candy, oh so sweet,
While dolphins dove down, flipping on their feet.
The sun wore shades, said, 'Cool, what a day!'
While sunbathers giggled, sunscreen on display.

A tiny boat rocked, like a child in thought,
As waves whispered secrets, caught and forgot.
Flip-flops did a tango, what a hot mess,
As chilled drinks spilled stories, in all of the stress.

Sailing Through Dreamy Mists

Sailboats chatted softly in the breeze,
While fish tossed a party, with jellybean tease.
Marshmallow clouds floated, donning a grin,
Creating a splash, oh let the fun begin!

Waves cheered on pirates with eyes full of glee,
As crabs threw confetti, dancing with glee.
Seashells held cards, dealt some quite funny,
While octopuses juggled, 'Aren't we so sunny?'

Surrender to Sweet Ocean Whispers

Breezes whispered wishes, secrets untold,
As starfish played poker, beaming and bold.
The horizon sparkled with laughter and cheer,
Where mermaids cracked jokes, 'You should come here!'

Beach balls bounced high, like dreams on a spree,
While seagulls debated who's the best spree.
Shells shared their tales, all were enchanted,
As the sun dipped low, its golden light granted.

Serenade of the Sandy Shores

The seagulls call with flair,
They steal my fries, I swear!
The waves tickle my toes,
While I dodge surfer woes.

A crab with a sideways strut,
Approaches my beach hut.
I offer him a snack,
He scuttles in a mad act.

Sunburnt noses all around,
Laughter echoing, so loud!
Flip-flops flying off our feet,
As we dance to a funny beat.

The sand sticks to my ice cream,
What a messy, melting dream!
With giggles under the sun,
We bask until the day is done.

Beneath the Coconut Canopy

Coconuts drop like surprise,
Always aiming for my eyes.
Next to me, a parrot squawks,
In this jungle, he just talks.

I sip juice from a bright cup,
With a tiny umbrella up.
Ants march in a single line,
Stealing crumbs, oh that's divine!

Laughter bounces off the leaves,
I wear a crown of palm, who believes?
Bumbling bees buzz with glee,
While I try to climb a tree!

A bat flies by with a squeak,
Making my cool drink leak.
Underneath this leafy shade,
The best fun is surely made!

Dances of the Evening Fireflies

Fireflies blink like disco balls,
They twinkle, dance, and make me fall.
In the garden, we spin and sway,
Ignoring bugs that come to play.

My friends trip over summer shoes,
With laughter mixing with sweet hues.
A frog croaks out a silly tune,
While the stars peek out like a balloon.

I attempt a graceful twirl,
And step into a mystery whirl.
With giggles echoing through the night,
The moon laughs at our silly sight.

So we sway until we tire,
Chasing dreams fueled by ire.
As fireflies whisper goodnight songs,
In this dance, where all belong.

Waves Caress the Quiet Hearts

The ocean whispers secrets here,
While I dodge a crab with cheer.
A wave rolls in, kisses my feet,
Flipping me over, what a treat!

Seashells scatter with a chime,
I find one that's quite sublime.
A fish jumps up, gives a grin,
With a splash, the game begins!

The breeze brings laughter near,
As we float, taking a beer.
Mermaids chuckle from afar,
Winking at our silly spar.

As daylight fades, we sing loud,
Proud of laughter that we've vowed.
The waves caress our restless hearts,
In this joy, the fun never departs!

Aroma of Exotic Blooms

In a garden where funny smells blend,
A flower sneezes, it's hard to pretend.
The roses throw a party on the vine,
And tulips gossip over a glass of wine.

A bee comes buzzing with a silly dance,
Distracting blooms in a vibrant trance.
They laugh so hard, their petals shake,
A daisy jokes, "I think I've lost my stake!"

Sailors of the Soft Sea Breeze

Imagine sailors on a wobbly boat,
They tip and they laugh, like a floating goat.
With hats flying high, they start to sing,
While fish below do a wiggly fling.

One sailor says, "I'll catch lunch with style!"
A fish jumps up and they giggle a while.
"More bait, less clumsiness!" they jest,
As seagulls swoop down, it's truly a fest!

Shadows of the Rustling Palms

Underneath palms where shadows play,
A lizard struts in a most charming way.
It wiggles and jiggles, a true superstar,
Singing to crickets from afar.

The winds whisper secrets, making them frown,
As coconuts tumble, trying not to drown.
"Who made this mess?" the palms start to shout,
While the lizard just giggles and prances about!

Hymn of the Rising Sun

The sun peeks up, all sleepy and round,
It yawns so wide, it nearly falls down.
A rooster crowing, a morning delight,
His chest puffed out, oh what a sight!

The clouds join in, with shapes all around,
Making funny faces, that's newly found.
The sun chuckles softly at the playful crew,
Saying, "Let's rise up, there's much fun to do!"

Lengthy Shadows of Late Afternoon

The sun leans low on sandy shores,
Where flip-flops dance and laughter roars.
A crab in shades with style so fine,
Steals clams with grace, oh, what a crime!

Palm trees giggle as breezes play,
Whispers of sunburned folks at bay.
A piña colada spills on knees,
While seagulls laugh, flying with ease.

Waves Cradling Soft Aching Hearts

The surf rolls in with a playful grin,
As lovers chase dreams like waves that spin.
A dolphin leaps in a splashy show,
While sunscreen fights against the glow.

Umbrellas waving in joy and fright,
As children argue who holds the kite.
Sandcastles crumble, yet spirits soar,
With each gentle wave, there's always more.

Soiree of the Nightingale's Call

A moonlit dance on a beach so fine,
With crickets chirping, it's party time!
Coconuts sway and gossip like friends,
While fireflies twinkle, their light never ends.

The nightingale sings of love's sweet plight,
As owls hoot back, keeping time just right.
A rhythm of laughter, with drinks in hand,
Under stars we sway, the happiest band.

Tides That Write Our Stories

Each wave that crashes brings tales anew,
Of sunburned pirates and mermaids too.
The tide draws pictures in sand so bright,
While seagulls cackle at love in flight.

With every breeze, our follies appear,
Like flip-flops lost in a game of cheer.
Seashells echo our giggles and sighs,
As tides tickle truth from playful lies.

A Canvas of Painted Skies

In hues of laughter, moonbeams dance,
The sun spills lemonade at every chance.
Palm trees sway in a funky beat,
While flip-flops orchestrate this retreat.

Seagulls steal fries, it's all in good fun,
A bright beach ball darts, like a playful pun.
Waves giggle, splashing its neighbor's hat,
As sunburned tourists look for shade—oh, that!

Crabs in tuxedos, a crabby charade,
While piña coladas put worries on parade.
The seashore whispers tales of delight,
As sunscreen becomes the day's fashion right.

With each sunset, the canvas ignites,
A portrait of joy, in silly delights.
And under the stars, we'll laugh 'til we cry,
In this playful paradise, where giggles fly.

Journey Through the Isles of Enchantment

Where coconuts chuckle and parrots play tricks,
   Hopping in boats with only two oars to fix.
A treasure map drawn in ketchup and fries,
   Exploring the isles with fishy surprise.

Mermaids gossip, tossing their hair,
While sun-kissed surfers develop flair.
Lost flip-flops become a new fashion trend,
As pineapple boats float, all comical bends.

Sandy toes wriggle, a tickling tease,
Magic wands made of driftwood and cheese.
Lover's quarrels brought on by misplaced tan,
In the glow of the dusk, they dance hand in hand.

Giggles drift high, on the winds of the seas,
Amid towering crabs, waving palm trees.
And when they stumble, they trip like no other,
In this whimsical land, joy is their mother.

Colors of an Endless Summer

On a canvas of sun, where giggles reside,
Skateboards flirt with the river's cool glide.
Jumping in puddles of spilled fruity drinks,
As ducks waddle by, giving us winks.

Sun hats tipping, with shades all askew,
Ice cream drips down; it's a sticky debut.
Children giggle in mud, as they race,
The winner yells loud, sporting chocolate face.

A shuffleboard duel, with laughter and cheer,
Competing in chaos, friends gather near.
The heat's so relentless, yet we dance on the shore,
As sandcastles rise up, demanding encore.

With kites at the ready, we soar skies aflame,
In vibrant hues, we're all part of the game.
Chasing the sunsets, we twirl and we dive,
An endless summer, where humor's alive.

Emotions Wrapped in Coral Lace

In coral dreams, where silliness grows,
Bubbles and giggles, like pink marshmallow snows.
A dance of sea cucumbers swaying in time,
As laughter unspools in a twisty rhyme.

Sassy seashells gossip, they talk behind backs,
While a jellyfish winks in its bright little slacks.
A fishy parade, with a splash and a flip,
Our beachside fiesta, a joyful trip.

With lemonade hugs in a coconut shell,
The warmth of the sun casts a humor spell.
Starfish dozed off, in funny repose,
Their dreams hold the secrets of ticklish toes.

And as the day fades, we giggle and sway,
In coral lace dreams, we frolic and play.
The tides hum a tune, so lighthearted and spry,
In this whimsical world, we float and we fly.

Lullabies Under the Starry Sky

Beneath the moon's warm, glowing light,
The crabs are dancing, what a sight!
A parrot sings a tuneful jest,
While coconuts put dreams to rest.

The breeze is chuckling, soft and sly,
A hammock sways, oh me, oh my!
The fireflies flicker, flashes bright,
As palm trees gossip through the night.

When roosters crow at dawn's first kiss,
The sleepyheads will surely miss
The chance to stretch and join the fun,
While chasing shadows of the sun.

So lift a drink, let laughter flow,
In this land where chuckles grow,
For every wave's a fitting prank,
In this paradise, we laugh and thank.

Tranquil Echoes of Island Time

With flip-flops slapping on the sand,
The sunburned tourists take a stand.
The seagulls laugh, they've got the knack,
To steal your fries and not look back.

Barefoot adventures, oh so sweet,
Fish tacos served, a tasty treat.
The local cat demands a scratch,
While eager crabs prepare to hatch.

Umbrellas twirl in playful dance,
While sunblock hides each sunburned chance.
A wave rolls in, a splash, a spin,
And laughter echoes, let's begin!

With every sunset's vibrant glow,
We bid farewell, but laughter's flow
Is stuck in time, forever here,
In island dreams, we hold so dear.

Petals Upon the Gentle Wind

A toucan tumbles through the trees,
Chasing petals with the breeze.
Each flower giggles, bright with cheer,
While butterflies are sipping beer.

The sun is warm, the drinks are cold,
The tales of palm trees, oft retold,
Lime and salt, a silly mix,
And coconut smiles for all the tricks.

The island airs are full of jest,
As every wave delights to rest.
In friendly banter, time flies high,
With sunburned cheeks and laughter nigh.

So take a nap or dance a jig,
The rhythm here is never big.
For petals swirl, and giggles play,
A symphony of joy each day.

Reflections in the Surging Tide

When tide rolls in, it brings the fun,
With beach ball battles 'til we're done.
The water splashes, giggles loud,
As seagulls mock a passing crowd.

A surfboard's stuck, the guy's a mess,
In every wave, a new caress.
Fish swim by, with playful winks,
While tourists ponder ocean drinks.

The sunset paints the skies in pink,
As mermaids gather, winks and clinks.
A starfish grins beneath the foam,
In salty depths, we find our home.

So let the tide keep rolling round,
With laughter as our joyful sound.
For each reflection holds a jest,
In this paradise, we find our rest.

The Lure of Distant Horizons

There's a beach where the seagulls chatter,
With umbrellas that bloom like flowers.
I tripped on my flip-flops, what a splatter!
While chasing a crab that reveals its powers.

Coconut drinks, oh what a delight,
They spill on my shirt like a wild night.
I smile at the sun, feeling quite bright,
Yet trip over sunbathers out of sight!

The waves play tag with my sunburned toes,
Each splash sends a giggle that joyfully flows.
I dodge a beach ball, how it glows,
In this quirky troupe where laughter grows.

A treasure chest filled with half-eaten snacks,
Rummaged by seagulls, they show no lacks.
A pirate hat made of snack pack backs,
In the ocean of fun, we've all got the knack.

Embrace of the Saltwater Kiss

Oh the ocean's embrace is a slippery thrill,
With salt on my lips and fish that stand still.
I danced with a wave, got knocked down the hill,
Now I'm covered in sand and tasting the chill.

Seashells like treasures, I pick them with glee,
One whispers secrets, it tickles my knee.
A crab photobombs, oh, what a sight to see!
Looks like my selfie now hosts a decree.

The gulls squawk loud, they plan out a feast,
Snatching my popcorn, what blundering beasts!
I try to resist, yet they laugh like a beast,
While I sit and ponder, at least not the least.

In the frothy surf, I found my old shoe,
An adventurous ride where the antics just grew.
A splash and a slip, oh how irony flew,
But at the end of the day, I'm still laughing too!

Moonlit Paths through the Dunes

Under a moon that winks like a star,
I tripped over dunes while chasing a car.
A vision so bright, yet here we are,
With sand on my face, and the waves that spar.

The crickets sing tunes of mischief and mirth,
As I slide down the dunes, oh what a birth!
A tumble and giggle, what joy to unearth,
Finding my flip-flops, it's chaos and worth.

Stars twinkle above like sequins in flight,
As ghosts of the beach give a ghostly light.
I dare to make friends with a crab, what a fright,
Turns out he just wanted to join in the night.

In the whisper of waves, moonlit paths gleam,
We wave to night critters, like a strange dream.
Embracing the tripping and falling, it seems,
The laughter stays strong, like a wild, silly beam.

Rhythms of the Coconut Hammock

In a hammock that sways with a curious tune,
I nap like a sloth, til I swoon and balloon.
A coconut lands, boo! What a rude boon,
And my sandwich decides to elope with the moon.

Swaying and dancing, a rhythm so spry,
While sipping my drink and wondering why.
A gecko's my partner, we both get high,
But then I fall out, oh dear me, oh my!

The palm trees are freely chatting away,
I feign sophistication, but lose it in play.
They rustle and laugh as I frantically sway,
In this hammock of giggles, the world's my buffet.

Counting my blessings, they dance on my chest,
With beach balls and joy, now I feel truly blessed.
The rhythms keep flowing, our laughter's the best,
In this haven of silliness, I'm never a jest.

Rhapsody of the Sunlit Isles

On a beach where coconuts fall,
Sunbathers slip, oh what a sprawl,
Seagulls squawk, just like my Aunt,
Offered her shade, but she can't grant.

Flip-flops lost in the sand's embrace,
A crab scuttles off, quickening the pace,
Pineapple drinks spill, oh what a mess,
But laughter grows, I can't help but confess.

Umbrella flies off, a kite in disguise,
Catching the wind and soaring the skies,
We chase it down, giggling with glee,
Who knew that beach days would be so free?

In the sun, all worries take flight,
Dancing with shadows till the night,
With playful hearts and sunburnt hides,
We toast to life, wherever it hides.

Secrets of the Lush Greenery

In a garden where the monkeys play,
Banana peels lead the wrong way,
A parrot squawks, oh what a show,
As I trip over roots, down I go!

Lush vines twist, a tangled ballet,
Finding my way is an artful cliché,
With mushrooms sprouting like fancy hats,
I ponder life while dodging the spats.

Frogs croak tunes like a jazz band gone wild,
Bees buzzing in rhythm, nature's own style,
A squirrel steals snacks, yes, he's the thief,
But laughter erupts, it's impossible to grieve.

Every corner hides a surprise or two,
A flower that giggles, a plant that's blue,
In this green maze, there's seldom a frown,
Just peals of joy wearing nature's crown.

Castaways in Paradise

Stranded here with a sandwich and drink,
No rescue boat, just time to think,
A palm tree leans, can I use it for shade?
But it's doing a dance, how rude and unmade!

Seashells whisper secrets of old,
Caught on the beach, feeling quite bold,
With coconuts rolling, they join in the fun,
Who knew being cast away was so pun?

A crab steals my flip-flop, a cheeky chap,
While sunbathers shuffle, time for a nap,
Every sunset brings a pirate's delight,
I wave my white flag, it's a party tonight!

In this haven of laughter, we take to the skies,
With dreams of fresh coconuts and spaghetti fries,
We may be lost, but with friends by our side,
Life's one big laugh, let's take it in stride.

Murmurs of a Midnight Lagoon

Underneath the glow of the stars,
Frog choirs croon from their slimy bars,
Waves shimmer softly, a gentle lull,
While fireflies twinkle, oh what a pull!

Rowing my boat with a plastic oar,
The fish poke their heads, asking for more,
Splashing around like they're in a race,
While I giggle awkwardly, splashed in the face.

A coconut floats by, an island delight,
I ponder if it's a friendly sight,
With laughter echoing through the night air,
A dance-off with crickets, if you dare!

Murmurs rise up like the tide in disguise,
In this midnight realm, we laugh and we guise,
With starry horizons and dreams anew,
Every moment's treasure, shared by the crew.

Reflections on Still Waters

The ducks are plotting in a row,
They've got their shades, ready for the show.
In perfect sync, they quack a tune,
A splashy dance beneath the moon.

Here come the frogs, in silly hats,
They ribbit loud, like silly chats.
Their leaps are wild, their jumps a jest,
Who knew the pond could be so blessed?

A fish in flip-flops floats by,
With sunglasses on and a carefree sigh.
"Life's but a splash," he seems to say,
In this wacky pond where ducks play.

At dusk, they drink from a fountain of mirth,
In their watery world, they know their worth.
Reflection gleams, the fun won't cease,
For in these still waters, there's always peace.

Whispers of the Ocean Breeze

The waves chat softly, a giggling crew,
They tickle the toes of the beach's view.
"Watch out!" they shout, as they start to race,
With foamy glee, they splash in place.

A crab in sunglasses struts with flair,
He does the cha-cha without a care.
Seashells chuckle, their secrets old,
In this dance of joy, laughter unfolds.

The seagulls soar in a comical flight,
Playing tag while chasing the light.
"Oy vey!" one shrieks, as he swirls around,
No worries here in this blissful sound.

As twilight descends with a wink and a nod,
The breeze whispers tales that feel quite prod.
Oh, what a party under the sun,
Where every wave brings more silly fun!

Palms in the Twilight

The palms sway softly, wearing a grin,
As the breeze tickles their leafy skin.
"Oh, look at that!" one palm beaned,
"I think the coconuts have all teamed!"

A troupe of coconuts starts a parade,
Rolling around in a nutty escapade.
They trip and tumble, what a sight,
In the shadowy glow of the fading light.

A squirrel dons a hat made of leaves,
Dancing with joy among the eaves.
"Let's bust a move!" he chirps with glee,
In this twilight world, come dance with me!

As stars peek out, they twinkle and tease,
The palms continue their sway with ease.
For in this twilight, the fun won't cease,
Life's a riot, just let it increase!

Echoes of Sunlit Dreams

Under the sun, a snail takes a stroll,
With shades on tight, he feels quite whole.
"Zoom zoom!" he mumbles, though slow he seems,
In a world where laughter fuels the dreams.

Nearby, a parrot tells a tall tale,
Of swimming with fish on a grand sail.
But the fish just giggle, scales all aglow,
As they play peek-a-boo in the currents below.

Sunflowers sway, joining the throng,
Singing sweet tunes to nature's song.
"All's well!" they hum, as bees buzz by,
In a land where happiness flutters high.

As daylight fades, a party ignites,
With shadows dancing in fun-filled nights.
In echoes of dreams, the joy cascades,
For in this realm, laughter never fades.

Embracing Sunsets

When the sun dips low, we cheer,
As if it's our friend, oh dear!
With drinks balanced high in the air,
We dance like we haven't a care.

Orange and pink paint the sky,
We laugh as seagulls fly by.
Each wave whispers salty delight,
In this joyous evening light.

Our toes in sand, we wiggle around,
Forget the chores that abound.
"Let's catch a wave!" someone shouts,
And we trade our worries for sprout-outs.

As the sunset bids its farewell,
We're plotting our next grand spell.
With smiles wide like the sea,
Who knew a sunset would set us free?

Fleeing Night

The sun has set, we flee in fright,
From shadows lurking in the night.
But wait, there's laughter in the breeze,
As we spot the party with ease!

Moonlight dances on our skin,
Who knew mischief would begin?
With ice cream cones melting away,
We giggle, plotting games to play.

"Hide and seek?" someone suggests,
In the sand, we'll be the best!
But stumbled feet and slippery heels,
Turn our giggles into squeals.

So bring on the stars, let's collide,
In a whirlwind; we'll take it in stride!
With each stumble, we'll laugh on cue,
For who needs night when we have our crew?

Wanderlust Beneath the Banyan Tree

Underneath the branches wide,
We sit, where all dreams abide.
A squirrel joins in with a grin,
As we share tales of where we've been.

Each story funnier than the last,
With antics that are unsurpassed.
We'll pretend we're explorers bold,
In lands filled with treasure untold.

But then a bug bites at my toe,
"No thanks!" I squeal, "I'm not feeling show!"
While friends just laugh, and roll with glee,
Caught in the whimsy of the tree.

With snacks we munch, both sweet and salty,
Under our canopy, so exalted!
We find our heartbeats quicken in glee,
As the world slows, just us and the tree.

Glimpse of Paradise in a Teardrop

Caught in a drizzle, oh what a sight,
Raindrops splatter, turning day bright.
A teardrop rolls down a cheek,
But wait—see the rainbow peek!

Laughter bubbles with every splash,
As puddles form in quite a dash.
We jump like kids, without a care,
Chasing giggles through the wild air.

A sudden gust takes our snacks away,
But laughter replaces the fray.
With sticky fingers, we embrace the fun,
In our own paradise, we've just begun!

So let the clouds do their worst,
In this moment, joy's first!
For every teardrop is just a chance,
To wildly laugh in this rain-dance!

Night's Embrace on Sugar Sands

The moon spills silver on sandy shores,
While we chase shadows, and laughter roars.
With friends nearby, what can go wrong?
We sing off-key in a silly song.

The tide softly tugs at our toes,
With every wave, another giggle grows.
Sandcastles crumble beneath our feet,
"Oh no!" we shout, "That's quite a feat!"

Beach blankets are tangled, oh my,
But who needs neatness when spirits fly?
With sleepy eyes and silly dreams,
We share whispers beneath the moonbeams.

As night embraces with a twinkling call,
We know together, we have it all.
So bring on the stars, let them shine bright,
For nothing's more fun than a perfect night!

Serenity in the Sun's Glow

Beneath the palms, we sip our drinks,
A seagull steals my sandwich, it thinks.
With laughter ringing, we toss the ice,
And dodge the waves like they're not so nice.

The sun is bright, our hats are wide,
We chase the crabs that scuttle and glide.
In flip-flops racing, I trip and fall,
It's just a splash, not a waterfall!

The coconut's sweet, the breeze is warm,
Yet here comes the breeze, such a charm!
With silly hats and sunscreen lathered,
The joy we find, oh how it mattered!

As day drifts by, the sunset glows,
And nighttime giggles begin to compose.
We dance like no one's watching, oh what a sight,
Our silly antics glow in the moonlight!

Flickering Shadows on Sandy Shores

The sun dips low, our shadows swell,
We draw stick figures, and ring a bell.
Laughter echoes like crashing waves,
While dodging splashes our heart misbehaves.

A beach ball bounces right off my head,
Landing near a sandcastle, so well spread.
With buckets and shovels, we sculpt and create,
But the tide comes running, oh isn't that fate?

The sunscreen's sticky, like glue on our arms,
A crab takes a roam, getting all of our charms.
With flip-flops flopping, our dive is grand,
Yet we flounder and sing, "We're the kings of the sand!"

As the stars appear in the night sky's hue,
We still chase the crabs, like kids with a coup.
Flickering laughter, oh what a delight,
On these sandy shores, everything feels right!

Crescendo of the Tropical Twilight

The sun is a painter, the sky is his canvas,
As night creeps in, everyone starts to panic.
With fruity drinks, we spin and sway,
The dance floor now calls, come on, let's play!

The tiki torches sway, with flames that flicker,
I dared to dance close, but fell on the snicker.
With limbo competitions, we all take a turn,
Yet one too many cocktails makes the balance burn!

The night wears a gown of sparkly stars,
And someone just shouted, "Where are my cars?"
With laughter we tumble, the sand feels so fine,
Yet we can't find shoes—was that a misdesign?

As fun takes a bow, the twilight is here,
With silly moments that stretch so clear.
In the glow of the night, our hearts twist and whirl,
In a crescendo of laughter, our joy starts to unfurl!

Fleeting Moments in Ocean's Arms

Splashing and laughing, we run from the tide,
But the waves can be cheeky; they nudge from the side.
With every dip, there's a squeal and a shout,
As the ocean giggles, we dance about!

We find a floaty shaped like a whale,
But it drags like a rock, much too frail.
We giggle and flop, trying to glide,
Yet we look more like ducks in this watery ride!

The sun sets low, as we race to the shore,
With shells in our pockets and sand evermore.
Yet nobody warned of the jellyfish sting,
We leap and we laugh, like it's all a grand fling!

As the day whispers secrets, we gather around,
With fleeting moments, sweet joy can be found.
So here's to the silliest times by the sea,
In the arms of the ocean, we're totally free!

Delicate Threads of Sunset Tides

The sun dips low with a splash and swirl,
A crab in a tuxedo gives it a whirl.
Seagulls squawk at the fading light,
As dolphins giggle in sheer delight.

Flip-flops dance on the sandy floor,
While beach balls bounce and soar.
A sunburned guy lounges in bliss,
Dreaming about the tan he'll miss.

Children chase shadows, laughter in air,
As the tide creeps up, oh, what a scare!
With ice cream dripping down all sides,
The joy of summer in silly rides.

In the twilight glow, a firefly appears,
Lighting up hopes and silly fears.
A sunset so grand, it whispers, "Hey!"
Every smile counts at the end of the day.

Fluttering Hopes in the Warmth

A butterfly flutters, no care in sight,
Winging its way through the golden light.
Sandcastles rise like dreams untold,
While seagulls plot to steal the gold.

The breeze plays tricks, a mischievous game,
As hats take flight, it's hard to tame.
Laughter erupts where the waters meet,
With a splash from the dog that can't feel his feet.

Kids run in circles, in brightly striped gear,
Chasing each other, igniting cheer.
A hidden treasure waits in a shoebox,
Containing mostly seaweed and some old socks.

In the warmth, where the sun shines bright,
Every little mishap feels just right.
With ice-cold drinks and friends nearby,
Every moment is worth a silly sigh.

Silence Between the Palm Leaves

Palm leaves whisper secrets so sweet,
While crickets perform with a tap on their feet.
In the hush of night, a coconut drops,
Right on the head of the guy who hops.

Laughter bubbles up like joy in the night,
As a wandering cat claims its rightful bite.
The moon grins down from a stage up high,
While stars flare up like popcorn in the sky.

A hammock sways, a kiss of the breeze,
As marshmallows toast 'round the nighttime tease.
Friends gather 'round with stories to weave,
While the ocean laughs at what we believe.

In the stillness, moments softly glide,
Making memories on this carefree ride.
With smirks and snickers, mischief in play,
The night dances on in a bright array.

Island Echoes in the Stillness

Echoes of joy bounce off the shore,
As laughter floats out, a melodic score.
Coconuts clatter on the sun-warmed sand,
Creating a rhythm that's perfectly grand.

Boozy drinks shake like a maraca's sound,
As friends unleash shenanigans all around.
With sun hats turned upside-down on their heads,
Every moment now rife with droll spreads.

Echoes of parrots shout, "Polly wants more!"
While chipper fish peek and explore.
The warmth of the island brings giggles anew,
Under palm trees swaying with a spectacular view.

In stillness, happiness dances like the tide,
With jokes from the heart that nobody can hide.
The echoes remind us, in laughter we find,
The joys of the islands, all intertwined.

Whirling Dervishes of the Dawn

The roosters crow, they twist and twirl,
A dance of feathers in a morning swirl.
Coffee brews like lava flow,
Who thought mornings could steal the show?

Bananas slip on polished floors,
Dancers tripping through open doors.
The sun peeks in with a cheeky grin,
While parrots shout, "Let the fun begin!"

The waves will join this joyful spree,
Tickling toes, just wait and see.
A conga line of beach ball dreams,
Dance with mermaids, or so it seems.

Oh, swirling shapes beyond the bay,
Who knew mornings could be this play?
As laughter spreads on ocean tides,
Life's a carnival, oh what rides!

Vibrations of the Coral Heart

Underwater, fish make quite the scene,
Their little flippers flash and gleam.
Coral giggles, oh what a sight,
Fish throwing parties every night!

Sea turtles dressed in style and grace,
Wrinkled legends in a joyful race.
They shimmy and shake with a wink,
While starfish giggle, what do you think?

Octopuses juggling shells with charm,
Waving their arms, causing no alarm.
The bubbles dance, oh how they rise,
While crabby critters trade surprise pies!

In this funny world under the sun,
Life's an art, for everyone.
The coral heart beats bold and loud,
A raucous party, let's all be proud!

Kaleidoscope of Island Colors

Paint the sky in shades of cheer,
With pinks and blues that twirl and smear.
Palm trees sway in a polka-dot show,
While coconuts drop, but oh, take it slow!

The sunset glows like a giant smile,
Mermaids brushing their scales with style.
Rainbows arch with a silly twist,
Guiding laughter, impossible to resist.

Lizards in hats, oh what a sight,
Join the fun, day turns to night.
With colors swirling in joyous delight,
Every moment feels just right!

Life's a canvas, what fun to paint,
With laughter and joy, let's not faint.
In every hue, there's mischief, it seems,
A kaleidoscope of funny dreams!

Heartbeats of the Uncharted Islands

In waters deep, the silly fish swim,
With swaying fins, they take a whim.
Each heartbeat pulses, a rhythm of glee,
Oh, what a party, come splash with me!

Seagulls gossip on the golden shore,
Trading stories of treasure and lore.
Sandcastles crumble, but fear not the fate,
For every collapse makes room for a great rate!

The wind-twisted tunes make palm leaves sway,
As laughter spills out, come join the play.
Hidden spirits, with mischief abound,
In every echo, joy is found!

So step on this path of the unknown,
Where heartbeats dance and laughter's grown.
The uncharted beats call out your name,
Let's dive into fun, we'll never be the same!

Vibrant Hues of Paradise

In a land where the colors bloom,
The parrots dance and the flowers loom.
A pineapple hat on a coconut head,
They sip their drinks while lying in bed.

With shades so bright, they can blind a goat,
Laughter bubbles in a small little boat.
A crab in a tux, he waddles with glee,
Inviting all fish for a beachside tea.

Banana peels scattered like stars,
A mischief-maker under the bars.
With flip-flops flying through the warm air,
Who knew paradise holds so much flair?

The sunset comes wearing pink and gold,
A tale of joy waiting to be told.
Sandals squeak as the party takes flight,
In this vibrant land, everything's right.

Ebbing Tides of Delight

Waves chuckle as they dance on the shore,
A jellyfish jiggles while asking for more.
Starfish giggle at the tickling tide,
As crabs play tag and laugh side by side.

Seagulls squawk jokes from the skies above,
Each feathered friend bursting with love.
Flip a fish like a pancake, real quick!
Underwater pranks make the ocean tick.

Shells whisper tales of the pranks they've seen,
A mermaid grins, her face lit and keen.
As the sun dips low in the ocean so wide,
Find a sea cucumber clutching its pride.

The moonscape lights with a silvery glow,
As the waves take a break, putting on a show.
Night brings a shimmer and the laughter resounds,
With ebbing tides of joy, our glee knows no bounds.

Songs from the Coastal Heart

A ukulele strums 'neath the palm so bright,
As locals gather for a joyful night.
With hula moves and a coconut smile,
They bring out the fun, hang around for a while.

The tide brings songs of the dolphin choir,
With each splash, they lift spirits higher.
A crab does the cha-cha, shells in a row,
While a parrot croons, putting on a show.

In the distance, a conch shell begins to hum,
A turtle joins in, keeping the rhythm fun.
Belly flops echo; it's time for a dive,
These coastal tunes make the heart come alive.

With laughter erupting like bubbles in air,
Every twirl and twist, nothing to compare.
Songs from the heart, in the salt-kissed breeze,
Join the laughter and dance with such ease.

Sunkissed Dreams in Paradise

Under umbrellas, the secrets unfold,
With stories of llamas and glittering gold.
A sunburnt tourist loses his shoe,
Chasing his hat, oh what a view!

Tanned and twisted, folks lounge on the sand,
While a seagull steals fries, so unplanned.
Beach balls collide, laughter goes boom,
In this quirkiness, there's always room.

Ice cream drips like melted delight,
While sandy toes wiggle, buoyant and bright.
The sun plays tricks, casting shadows in jest,
A beach day like this surely is the best.

As twilight whispers the end of the play,
Stars twinkle - a cosmic cabaret.
In sunkissed dreams where giggles reside,
Life flows like waves, with joy as our guide.

Vows Made Under the Altar Sky

In sandals bright, we pledge our fate,
With coconuts as best mates.
The seagulls squawk, they steal the show,
As we laugh through love's sweet woe.

The tide rolls in, with mischief grand,
Our vows get swept, like grains of sand.
We stumble back, our hair a mess,
Two hearts, one sun, it's all excess!

A Lament for Lonely Beaches

Oh, lonely shores, you call my name,
With no one here, it's quite the game.
The flip-flops mock, they dance around,
While crabs and I scout for lost ground.

A turtle grins at my sad plight,
He'd wave, but it's a tiring flight.
I throw a shell; it bounces back,
No message found, just ocean's knack!

Each Grain Tells a Story

A grain of sand with tales to share,
Of flip-flop trips and summer air.
Each tiny speck, a laughter low,
A secret kept, that tides will blow.

They whisper tales of beachside feasts,
Of silly dances and hungry beasts.
I pluck one out, say, "Tell me more!"
But all it says is, "Get off the shore!"

Heartstrings Tugged by Ocean Currents

Oh, salty breeze, you tease my heart,
With waves that laugh, they take apart.
A fishy kiss, a splashy prank,
I frown at tides, they skip and yank.

With jellyfish as party crashers,
My swim's a dance of silly splashes.
Heartstrings tug beneath surf's charm,
As I lose my flip-flop, sinking calm!

Emerald Canopies and Mellow Mists

In the jungle high and bright,
Monkeys swing left and right,
With a laugh and a shout,
They play without a doubt.

Parrots squawk, a colorful cheer,
As fluttering leaves draw near,
But wait! Who's that in disguise?
A goat in shades, oh what a surprise!

Waves of green sway to the beat,
Of tiny feet that can't be beat,
In playful frolics, they align,
Nature's jesters, oh how divine!

Underneath the leafy dome,
Every creature feels at home,
With giggles, squirms, and tasty bites,
Emerald fields and mellow nights.

The Dance of Warm Winds

Warm winds whip through sun-kissed hair,
A parrot steals my lunch with flair,
While coconut shells tap dance on ground,
To the comical beats that abound.

Laughter echoes through the trees,
As crabs scuttle with such ease,
They're wearing hats made from old leaves,
Each strut a joy that never deceives.

A chubby iguana takes a turn,
Displaying moves we live and learn,
With a shimmy and a shake, oh geez!
He brings all of us to our knees!

In gusty breezes, life feels right,
As critters join our silly night,
With every twirl, a giggle reigns,
Where fun and warmth flow through our veins.

Coconut Lullabies and Starlit Nights

Under starlit skies so bright,
Coconuts fall left and right,
Each thud a sleepy serenade,
While crickets play, their voices cascade.

Seashells whisper secrets untold,
Of beachy tales and treasures of old,
While a crab with a sax joins the show,
Playing tunes that ebb and flow.

Fireflies dance with vivid lights,
A jolly sight on lazy nights,
With giggles shared, our worries fade,
As melodies of laughter invade.

In the calm, the world feels grand,
With silly stories hand in hand,
We drift to dreams, as stars take flight,
Under coconuts, our hearts ignite.

Beneath the Mango Tree's Embrace

In the shade of a mango tree,
Laughter bounces, wild and free,
As giggling kids come tumbling down,
With sticky hands and faces brown.

An ant parade marches by,
With tiny hats and numbers high,
They weave in patterns, oh so grand,
As popular as a rock band!

A wise old turtle takes a seat,
To share his tales, both strange and sweet,
While bees conduct a buzzing choir,
Encouraging dreams that never tire.

So under branches thick and wide,
We discover joy we cannot hide,
In the heart of nature, we find our place,
Beneath the mango tree's embrace.

Whispers of the Island Breeze

A coconut fell with a thud,
It missed my head by a hair,
I laughed as I dodged it quick,
Nature's way of showing flair.

The parrot squawks a cheeky tune,
A melody mixed with a tease,
He tells me jokes from noon to noon,
While I sip on rum with ease.

The sun's hot kiss made me a snack,
A sunburned nose, quite the sight,
I dance like a fool, no looking back,
Island life feels just so right.

As the hammock sways with a grin,
I ponder why I ever left,
I'd trade the world just to begin,
Another day, oh what a heft!

Sun-kissed Serenade

The sunbeams dance on my belly,
As I try to find my shade,
Flip-flops squeak, oh so silly,
I'm the jester on this stage.

A game of beach ball in full swing,
The seagulls laugh at my fall,
I land with flair, it's worth the sting,
Just another day, after all.

My ice cream drips with every lick,
A race against the melting sun,
With sprinkles flying, what a trick,
How did my treat become so fun?

But when the sun decides to dip,
I find my courage in the breeze,
A silly dance with every flip,
Life's a party, if you please!

Palm Shadows at Dusk

In the evening glow, I play a prank,
My buddy swipes my last cold drink,
He stumbles back into the plank,
Splashing water—oh, what a stink!

The palms sway gently in the laugh,
Casting shadows on the sand,
The sunset's painting a silly graph,
Of a giant fish with a band.

As stars peek out with a wink,
We roast marshmallows on a stick,
The sand plays tricks, it makes me think,
Why do we love to play the trick?

I'll take this moment, so absurd,
Each giggle carried on the breeze,
With every joke, the magic stirred,
In palm shadows, we find ease.

Lullabies of the Ocean's Edge

The waves hum softly, what a tune,
A lullaby for the silly souls,
I watch the crabs dance under the moon,
In funny hats, they take their strolls.

A jellyfish floats, all fancy and bright,
With a crown made of starry light,
While fish below giggle all night,
In their underwater delight.

The tide rolls in with a splashy cheer,
I giggle as I slip in the foam,
A mermaid waves, she knows I'm here,
Inviting me to stay as home.

So let the ocean sing its song,
Where laughter mingles with the tide,
In this silly world, we belong,
With each wave, we take the ride.

A Symphony of Soft Waves

The ocean giggles, splashing bright,
Seagulls dance, quite a silly sight.
Shells whisper jokes beneath the sun,
Waves laugh loud, oh what fun!

Palms sway, waving their green hands,
Breezy laughs across the sands.
Crabs sidestep in a funny parade,
Joking with each flip and trade.

Flip-flops flung, a comical match,
Sandy toes, a carefree scratch.
Each wave rolls in with a teasing sigh,
Watch out, here comes a splash - oh my!

Under the sun, we've lost all fear,
Sandcastles crumble, yet we cheer.
A symphony made of laughter's cheers,
Ocean's humor sings for years.

The Scent of Salted Memories

A whiff of seaweed? What a treat!
Sandy snacks make the day complete.
Laughter drifts on the salty air,
Is that a dolphin? More like a bear!

Sunburns painting each back red,
Sunscreen wars, who'll lose their head?
A bucket of fun spills memories sweet,
As laughter fills the space beneath our feet.

Yummy ice cream melts down our hands,
Dripping tales of far-away lands.
Funny faces in the evening glow,
Stories rise like the tide, you know?

Seashells whispering tales so quaint,
Mermaids chuckling while we faint.
With each salty breeze comes joyful muse,
Collective giggles, we just can't lose!

Radiant Echoes of Nature's Hearth

Beneath the sun, the laughter tumbles,
Parrots chat, while the squirrelumbles.
In the trees, a party of eyes,
Nature's joke? Don't be too wise!

Coconuts dropping, a reluctant plop,
Lizards racing, won't ever stop.
Grasshoppers leaping, what a sight,
Each jump a joke, like pure delight.

Frogs croak puns, as crickets chirp,
Dance with the breeze, let loose, let's burp.
Sunshine beams through leaves so green,
A radiant stage, where fun's a routine!

As evening falls, stars join the game,
Each one twinkles, calling your name.
Nature chuckles, there's no end in sight,
Together, we laugh until the night.

Dappled Light and Gentle Waves

Dappled sunlight, a playful dance,
Waves tickle toes, making us prance.
Shadows giggle under palm trees,
Whispers of fun on a light breeze.

Surfboards clash, a wild jest,
Balance beams like a circus test.
With each wipeout, laughter grows,
Water fights? Now, that's how it goes!

The sun socks us with golden rays,
Making funny faces through the haze.
Caboose of fun on a sandy track,
Don't look now, here comes a whack!

Gentle waves with comedic spins,
Together we splash, lose our fins.
With all these chuckles and playful ways,
Our hearts sway to nature's laid-back plays.

Sailing on a Sea of Exiled Dreams

A ship set sail on a cereal box,
With spoons as oars and milk for docks.
Fish in sunglasses wave goodbye,
As we float on dreams that never die.

Pirates with capes made of old bedsheets,
Chasing down jellybean treats.
We sing sea shanties to the seagull choir,
While snacks are our treasure, we never tire.

The compass spins, our map a joke,
As we frolic with dolphins, trying not to choke.
A mermaid giggles, flipping her tail,
We tip our hats and set up sail.

The horizon shimmers with wobbly glee,
In a land where all snacks are gluten-free.
With every wave, a chuckle or two,
On this sea, the dreams come true!

Alchemy of the Celestial Waters

Moonbeams mix with tea and toast,
A cauldron of laughter, we love the most.
Stars drop in like giggling friends,
In this potion where hilarity never ends.

Fish toast parties and jelly donut moons,
We dance with the crabs to silly tunes.
A parrot with jokes perched on the ledge,
Mixing starlight at the water's edge.

We stir up giggles in shimmering bowls,
While seaweed gives high-fives to our souls.
The recipe calls for starry delight,
As we sip on the waves under the glorious night.

In this alchemy, we float and glide,
With bubbles of joy, our silly ride.
Every drop is a treasure, every sip a cheer,
With the moon as our bartender, we have no fear!

Jaded Shores and Wandering Souls

Footprints swirl like dancing spoons,
As we embark on adventures that loom.
The sand tickles toes, we laugh and fall,
While our shadows stretch, having a ball.

Seashells gossip about the last wave,
While crabs do the cha-cha, oh how they rave!
Beach balls zoom, they bounce and fly,
As seagulls swoop and join in the fly-by.

A beach hut sings songs of days gone past,
With old flip-flops that never last.
We sip coconut drinks with silly straws,
While sticky hands applaud with great applause.

As the sun sets low, we build castles high,
With sandy moats where dreams can fly.
These jaded shores hold laughter's embrace,
Wandering souls finding their place.

Sunbeams Dancing on Far-off Waves

Sunbeams boogie on the ocean floor,
While we wiggle and giggle, always wanting more.
The waves clap hands, a rhythmic cheer,
Inviting our hearts to dance like a deer.

We wear laughter like hats made of flowers,
Playing leapfrog with jellyfish for hours.
Crabs in tuxedos strut their stuff,
While turtles roll their eyes, laughing tough.

A coconut teapot brews wishes for fun,
As we jump over rainbows, two by one.
The surf's silly serenade makes us sway,
While we tumble and tumble in a playful ballet.

With every splash, a giggle erupts,
As fish in tuxedos act like grown-ups.
In this world of whimsy, joy waves its wand,
Beneath the sunbeams, our laughter responds.

www.ingramcontent.com/pod-product-compliance
Lightning Source LLC
Chambersburg PA
CBHW072131070526
44585CB00016B/1633